T0386024

My Holiday

Written by Shirin Yim Bridges

To Spain!

1st March

Dear Grandad,

We took Max to the kennel yesterday. Then we left! It took three hours to get to Spain!

Sam

Lots to See

3rd March

Dear Grandad,

We went out for three hours this morning. There was lots to see. I liked the horses.

Sam

A Festival

5th March

Dear Grandad,

We went to a festival yesterday. We danced for six hours!

Sam

The Beach

6th March

Dear Grandad,

We are on the train now. The train can go fast. We will be at the beach in one hour!

Sam

A Spanish Dress

7th
March

Dear Grandad,

We are going shopping
this afternoon.
Mum is going to get me
a Spanish dress!

Sam

Yum!

8th March

Dear Grandad,

We had lots of Spanish food tonight. Yum! We have a long train trip in the morning.

Sam

Up a Tower

9th
March

Dear Grandad,

We visited this church today.
We waited for an hour
to go up the tower.

Sam

See You Soon!

11th March

Dear Grandad,

It is our last night in Spain. We have had lots of fun! See you and Max soon.

Sam

Greetings from Spain